"Hope I Don't See You for A Long Time"

A unique and fun view from "Over-the-Counter"

Randall Wright, R.Ph.

Copyright © 2009 by Randall J. Wright

All rights reserved. Published in the United States by Summit Press, a division of Summit Speakers, LLC, Fairway, Kansas

Library of Congress Cataloging-in-Publication Data
Randall J. Wright

ISBN 978-0-578-02876-7
TXu 1-606-228

Printed in the United States of America

Design by Sue Breckenridge

10 9 8 7 6 5 4 3 2 1

First Summit Press Edition

                      Summit Press
                         Fairway, KS

Foreward

When the publisher sent me this manuscript to review, I was uncertain how I could possibly provide insight or commentary on the writings of a pharmacist. However, as I began to read, my eyes were opened, not to the science of medicine and chemical compounds, but to a rare art of interaction with humanity. Wright's insight is positively a joy to experience. He shares his personal experiences as one of the unsung professionals who quietly and soberly affect our lives, and he reveals how we, as patients, affect theirs. He touches not only the soul of the professional, but of the patient. His stories of how the depths of life, laughter, and love can enter the doors of a pharmacy and be deposited at the counter for introspection and contemplation bring forth an unexpected and inspiring perspective.

This book not only touched my heart; it brought a profound smile to my soul. It has challenged me to look twice at those whom I interact with, to take that extra moment and reflect upon their trials, heartaches, and pains — to reach out and dispense more than just a quick verse or prayer — to actually connect with them in ways that will bridge our lives with hope, joy, and peace.

Take the time to reflect upon the true art of human interaction. Being a professional not only means being good at what you do; but how you do it with class and character.

I invite you to turn the page, and when you reach the last, put it in a place where you can return to it from behind the counters of your own lives.

Enjoy. I certainly did.

Ken Duke, Pastor
Coquille, Oregon

Acknowledgements

These stories have stumbled around my head and heart, some for years. A number of people are responsible for getting them out and onto paper.

Bob Mobley went from a grammar checker to just the right person, at the right time, to say the right words. Then one night at book club with Jim and Ruth Siress, Sally and Paul Jenkins, Dan and Sherri Cram, Shawn and Conrad Jones, Anne and Chris Jones, and Claudia Wellman, he asked me to read some of my stories. They all listened, read, commented, and encouraged.

My good friends, Chris and Pam Bacon said they enjoyed them, Chris in his understated way and Pam in her effusive way. Then my sister-in-law Carolyn went superlative on me. Sheila Connolly, a pharmacist and friend, nodded her approval.

All this time, my friend Jean Dreiling would read them, sometimes just as I finished them, offering encouragement and a couple of spot-on suggestions. And my friend, Gretchen Robinson after getting a few rough copies via late-night e-mail, called early the next morning! Maggie Choplin liked them (no small recognition due to her healthcare background and being a long time friend). Valerie Stallbaumer, my longest friend, told me to write more.

Then Janet Conner, the only professional writer I know, after editing a number of the stories sent an e-mail: "I've enjoyed reading your book." Whoa. I almost went out and bought a beret, scarf, and a bottle of absinthe.

Sue Breckenridge, on more than one occasion, has taken what I have written and made it look like it is worth reading.

And all of these people would never have read what they did had it not been for Recie Mobley. Everyone should meet a Recie if they want to develop additional skills. First it was speaking, now it is writing. Thanks, Recie.

Randall Wright, R.Ph.

Table of Contents

FOREWARD

ACKNOWLEDGEMENTS

PREFACE

Hope I Don't See You for a Long Time............................1
At Least Jesse James Had a Gun 3
The Cog I Am 4
Lazarus 5
The Wages of Sin...7

LIFE — *Illustration by Sally Jenkins* 9
Voices 11
The Queen of Cool 12
Brand Name Dad 13
Baby with Colic 15
The Other Thing..16
A Lot of Pain 17
Sales 101: Insulin Syringes for Grandma..........................20
Herpes and the New Boyfriend 22
The Altered Script 25
Stunning Beauty, Startling Behavior 27
The Cursing..29
3 am Misoprotal 31
Where Is "The Actress" 33
Plan B The Negotiator 35
Plan B An Errand 37
The Arrest...38

LAUGHTER — *Illustration by Jaden Mobley* 41
Plan B The Road Trip...43
3 a.m. Poem 45
Is There Anybody Smarter Back There?.............................47
Bipolar Lesson 49
Retin A 51
Viagra®..52
In Praise of Odd 53

Conversation, Not Salvage 56
Coca Cola Tattoo 58
No Answer..59
Vasectomy Couples..61
New Skin..63
Tell My Wife 65
Food from a Machine...67

LOVE 69
Late Night Bikini..70
Life and Love 72
"Ms Bardot, Would You Please Come to the Pharmacy?"..74
"Hon" 75
"I Will Pray for the *RJ's* Family" 77
Birthdays 79
"I'll Wait" 82
How Many Pills Will I Live 83
19 Medicines, 39 Pills 84
Air Hunger...86
The Last Prescription...87
Take Care 88
At Peace for A Day 90

Sometimes a pharmacy is a thrilling place to be.

Preface

At first, if your pharmacy experience is like mine, your work is more about the science — the facts and the knowledge, than about the people. Then, as our encounters accumulate and develop, we begin building relationships. We begin to talk to our patients, instead of at them. At times, these innumerable encounters give us more energy than they take. They do more than make us feel good. They move and inspire us. The result is an accumulation of experience that yields a deeper awareness of how to use our knowledge and how to share it.

We cannot be untouched by all of this. As time passes, we listen better, talk better, see more, and understand more. We improve the quality of the pharmacy experience. We develop. We change from a source of technical information into a gift for our patients and our community.

And our hearts grow.

This is presumptive of me to say, so I say it with caution: these stories expose the heart of pharmacy. We live in such a high tech society that high touch is, if not forgotten, then relegated to second-tier importance. These stories show that knowledge and caring matter. Where you find one, there is always a need for the other.

Presumptive or not, I'm sure some of these stories will resonate with you. We share many of the same experiences. What bonds us together is the impact we have on people — on patients. What we have in common is the effect people have on us. No one practices in a vacuum.

I hope you enjoy.

Randall Wright

"Hope I Don't See You for A Long Time"

At the end of every of every conversation there is a last impression. This last impression, along with the first impression, is what the person tends to remember in an otherwise commonplace conversation. If something extraordinary happens, like giving a spouse CPR, they remember the extraordinary act and not the last impression. In 33 years as a community pharmacist, I've given CPR twice. In the remaining near half million encounters, my impression was finalized by how I said good-bye.

I have ended my pharmacy conversations with: "Thanks", "Come again", "See ya later", "Hope you get better", "I'm sorry you're hurting", "I'll keep you in my thoughts", "Take care", "Drive careful", "Be careful", "Be well", "Stay well," and "Call if you have any questions," all of which are fine. They leave a nice last impression. Then one day, **"Hope I don't see you for a long time,"** popped out of my mouth. It was perfect. It said what I wished. After all, if I don't see them they are not sick or hurt. And it also did something for me; it told me that what I just did for them helped them. This reinforcement is a subtle, powerful and necessary fuel. *Being a pharmacist is demanding work.*

Prescription volume is increasing (and increasing!). So much pharmacology whizzes by with this increasing volume of patients. "Did I catch everything?" is as stressful a thought as it is a prayer. Allergies have to be noted with new fills and checked with refills.

Previous adverse reactions are checked against new medicines that may be similar, checked, and checked again to make sure the right medicine gets to the right patient. And while computers help, all they do is help. The computer is not blamed when an error is made. All these safety checks are interrupted by the incessant ringing of the phone or chiming of the drive-thru window (I have become Pavlov's slobbering dog.), and the patient with the question, or rash, or head lice, or fever, or constipation, or diarrhea, or headache, toothache, dog bite, broken insulin bottle, early refill request, or altered Vicodin script. All this comes with increasing frequency and patients who are upset because of expired insurance plans or higher co-pays, and of course, the demand of every person for "I want it now," when asked, "When would you like to pick this up?"

When I say, *"Hope I don't see you for a long time,"* the smile I get from the patient as the thought sinks in lightens the stress on both sides of the pharmacy counter. Sometimes.

Randall J. Wright

"At Least Jesse James Had A Gun"

I have started and stopped writing many times, picking up pen and letting the story flow, other times jotting down notes, always doing so because of an extreme behavior or moving encounter. There is a microcosm that exists in a retail pharmacy. Like a good novel, all the elements of drama are there: life, death, laughter, love, and dynamic characters.

A customer once said to me, "At least Jesse James had a gun." By saying this, he inadvertently gave me my first story. A no-nonsense farmer in the midwest, he was tall, sinewy, muscular, wore a John Deere cap and had just been diagnosed with mild high blood pressure. When he found out the price of his medicine (Dyazide, a mild diuretic), he looked at me over the small bottle of capsules standing between us on the pharmacy counter, mentioned something about the price of the pills compared to a bushel of wheat, pulled out his wallet, and said, "At least Jesse James had a gun."

I had no idea what to say. The year was 1975, and I was less than six months out of pharmacy school. His remark left me befuddled and by some odd stimulus, got me thinking about all that I see, hear and smell across the pharmacy counter. These experiences accumulated and I became aware that retail pharmacy is more than just the pharmacology that patients and their medicines represent.

The world is a stage, or so I have read. The stories that follow are a partial listing of experiences from one stagehand.

The Cog I Am

My patient takes his medicine right in front of me. He pops the lid, shakes out one dipyridamole 25 mg, tosses it in his mouth like a peanut, dry swallows the tiny red pill, and continues talking to me. No big deal to him. Very big deal to me. I am startled and try not to show it.

For the first time, I have seen someone take medicine I am responsible for dispensing. Until this moment, everything I have dispensed has been taken in the patient's home or car, out of sight — out of my sight. Watching him swallow the pill shows me why my presence is needed — the cog I am in the assembly line of health care. Five minutes before, that tablet had been sitting in a much bigger container on the pharmacy shelf with a thousand more. Two minutes before, it rested on a counting tray with a random number of other dipyradmole. Thirty seconds before, it was dropped in a vial with the rest of the month's supply. And now it is traveling in this man's body, beginning the journey it was made to take. Seconds from now that pill will be in his stomach; two minutes from now in his blood. Five minutes from now, it will have touched all his organs. While he is talking I am not listening. I am thinking, "Did I do everything I was supposed to?"

In that moment, the need for my presence suddenly became clear and my career was born. Schooling had been my embryonic phase where I was merely a bulge in the womb of the University of Kansas School of Pharmacy.

I am the final cog between a very trusting public and very potent chemicals.

Randall J. Wright

Lazarus

I thought he was dead. Yet, there he stands at the pharmacy counter like it's no big deal.

"Man, am I glad to see you!" I almost shout while quickly walking toward him.

"Well, I'm glad to see you too," he says.

"No. I really am glad to see you. I haven't seen you for months and was afraid you had died."

"Wow," he says, "I haven't seen you, but I just thought you were on a lot of vacations."

We laugh, as people do at reunions. He is my Lazarus back from the dead.

You may wonder why I just didn't look up his name in our files to see if he had been in, but I couldn't remember his name. I should have remembered his name. I could remember his medicines, medical condition, and two stories. He takes MS Contin 60 mg — one daily for severe pain and morphine sulfate immediate release 15 mgs — one up to three times a day for breakthrough pain. He has severe peripheral neuropathy. It is odd, but for some patients I can recall what they take easier than their names.

Nurses, dentists, physical therapists, and doctors have clinical memories of their patients as well. They also have the added contact of touching their patients. The only touching pharmacists generally do is shaking hands. Pharmacists make contact through conversation — talking and listening — most of which sound like banter: quick, brief, and topical. This "gift for gab" helps develop a heightened listening skill. The pharmacists that I know who are above average have developed their listening skills. It is amazing what they can be aware of after just a few words. They give the banter "direction" as they look for signs of medicine interactions, side effects, dosing errors, increased stress, dehydration, and more. They ask better questions and find more hints in the answers.

Such pharmacists improve the quality of the patient's experience. It is traceable; at first these conversations build familiarity, and with familiarity comes acceptance. Acceptance leads to anticipation. When patients come to the counter, they look to see if you are there. The final stage of trust is conquered when the patient wants to tell you a personal story. Stories are intimate history and history is part of a person's soul.

One night my Lazarus told me two stories. The first was about all of his friends who had died. For some he shared names, for others, how they died: drugs, car wrecks, motorcycles or "just too much booze." He told me about how for years he and his wife would play cards and drink with them. She too, was gone. He was the last. Then after a pause for memories, longing, and bafflement, he said, "If I had known I would have lived this long I would have taken better care of myself."

All I thought to say was, "I'm glad you made it."

"Sometimes I'm not. Sometimes I am," he said.

Which is the second story.

Sometimes pharmacy is a place where people reveal a bit of their soul.

The Wages of Sin

Pharmacy school is a lot of hard science: chemistry, biology, math, physics, clinical rotations, labs, kinetics, medicinal chemistry, pharmaceutics, pharmacology, pharmacology, and more pharmacology. All are capped off by a fun-filled two-day event called the state boards. Get 75 percent or better or you miss the opportunity to share all this hard science with patients.

By the end of five years you are loaded with information and equipped with a unique vocabulary. You are motivated and ready to catch drug-drug interactions, prevent drug–food interactions, recognize side effects, reduce drug contributing iatrogenic events, and generally intercede in misuse, overuse, and underuse. And that's just in the first year! With enthusiasm comes the confidence that knowledge of hard science offers. It makes you feel like you really can make a difference. And, in fact, you shouldn't get behind a pharmacy counter without that desire and the confidence to do so.

However, taking time to listen, talk, and teach patients sometimes results in an education that proves how useful hard science is not. One such situation happened to me some three months out of pharmacy school. I was working in a small drugstore, and an older farmer came in to get his first-line high blood pressure medicine — a mild diuretic. After filling it, I proceeded to explain (lecture) how he could reduce his medicine use, reduce the chance of side effects, save money, and better control his high blood pressure by eating less, eating better,

"Hope I Don't See You for A Long Time"

watching his salt, drinking less, and not smoking. I went on about how his medicine was a first-tier therapy, how it showed a health condition that would readily respond to a change in habits. I probably went on even more about how his family would appreciate all this, and well, you get the idea: blah, blah, blah, and blah. After I was done, this very courteous and understanding gentleman held the bottle of medicine in the air between us and told me he liked to eat, drink, and smoke. He told me he didn't need to exercise because he worked on a farm and had a hundred head of cattle. Then he, now teaching me, pointed the bottle at the ceiling. "Know why I buy this?" he asked. "This is the wage I pay for my eating and drinking and smoking sins." And he smiled and left.

Sometimes pharmacy is a confessional — a soft science place

Life

Portrait of Randall by Sally Jenkins long time professional and personal friend that helped me become a work of art.

"Hope I Don't See You for A Long Time"

Randall J Wright

Voices

*I*t's 3 a.m., Wednesday morning, the beginning of "hump day."

The pharmacy is quiet. You can hear its heartbeat: the hum of the lights, and the squeaks and creaks of the conveyor belt as it churns over rollers. The phones have not rung for awhile; patients have not been in for awhile. The noise of the day, like dust, has settled. The pharmacy takes on that just-after-a-snowfall quiet. (Think Van Morrison singing, "It's so quiet in here.")

The phone rings.

"Good morning, *RJ's*," I say — not forcefully as I would surrounded by noise, rather as a greeting when surrounded by calm.

"Are you the pharmacist?" she asks. I can barely hear her, so I push the volume button a few times.

"Yes, I am."

"Can you answer a question about a medicine?" Her voice is still a whisper even with added volume.

"Yes."

"Is Risperdal® for hearing voices?" She is whispering (not to disturb them?).

"Yes, it can be."

Very quietly she says, "Thanks."

Click.

What is your hump day like?

The Queen of Cool

Kids are cool, some more than others, but one was coolest of them all. My Queen of Cool was a gregarious, mischievous, wild-haired, flip-flop-wearing, laughing six-year-old. She was also teaming with head lice.

Her mother brings her in around 1:30 in the morning. The store is quiet — no music, no other patients. While leading them to the head lice remedies on the other side of the store, I get an eight-to-ten-foot lead before I hear her running behind me. The smacking of flip flops against linoleum tells me she is gaining fast. Just at the moment when she is directly behind me I do a quick turn, point my finger down at her and yell, "Bam!" She cracks up and immediately jumps to me. I sweep her up and with her long legs straddling my hip, I bring her and her mother to the head lice products. Her mother and I talk. The girl tucks her head in the crook of my neck, then out, then back again, holding her right hand under my chin and then moving it to the opposite side of my neck. This hug lasts a minute or two while I explain the directions to her mother. I put her down and she stands right beside me looking up.

I go back to the pharmacy thinking I may need a can of Rid™ myself with such close contact. *I also think retail pharmacy doesn't get any better than this.*

Brand Name Dad

*A*lways, he is twentyish and stands holding a note in his hand with one or two words: Motrin, Tylenol. The handwriting is usually a woman's, most likely the baby's mother and she got these names from a late night call to her doctor. The baby has a mild fever.

I show him the generic version, but if this is his first born he wants the brand name. This is a cute moment in pharmacy. (A cute moment is anything that makes me smile.)

"No," he'll say. "I better take the brand name."

He does so for two reasons and not necessarily in this order. Reason number one: He wants assurance. He has crossed into new territory. Motrin and Tylenol are names he knows. He wants something he knows, because lately he has been overwhelmed by unknowns — crusty belly button, diapers, lotions, mother's milk, and such tiny fingers and toes. Reason number two: He needs exactly what is written on the paper — it is not a good idea to surprise new mothers.

But he is not out of the woods yet. Pressing decisions still loom, decisions like what flavor. Waiting for a new dad to make this decision is another cute moment. They go through such anguish. It can and does take an inordinate amount of time to decide between cherry, grape, or bubblegum. Out of necessity, I have invented a way to hurry the process along as well as provide assurance.

"Which flavor?" I will ask.

If he doesn't answer with mild facial contortions, he will say, "I don't know."

I give unproven guidance. If the baby is a boy, I ask what his own favorite flavor is. "Pick that one for your boy," I say. "Like father, like son." If the baby is a girl, I ask about the mother's flavor of choice. "Pick that one," I say. "Like mother, like daughter." And yes, there have been times when new dad called home to ask new mom what her favorite flavor was. My method is an unproven predictor of the baby's favorite flavor, but it helps us get past the decision so he can go home, help take care of the baby, and explain his choice.

Once the flavor is picked, I go over the directions. I show him that the medicine has a dropper. The dose should be dropped in the baby's mouth ("That's why it is a dropper," I say.), not squirted in so it can be spit out. "Your baby has tiny toes and fingers and a tiny throat," I say. "Droppers are used to give drops." As we finish the lesson, I ask if this is his first. I already know the answer.

"Yes."

"What's the name?" I ask.

He tells me.

"How come that name?" There's a story. There is always a story.

"Congratulations," I say.

"Thanks," he says, stepping away from the counter.

Sometimes he will come back moments later to switch flavors. He will not always over-think decisions like this one. His actions are like over-steering when first learning to drive. He wants to do everything right. I will never see him as proud or bewildered as in this moment. He walks toward the door and I smile. "May you always be such a good father," I say quietly to no one.

Sometimes pharmacy is just a nice place to be.

Baby with Colic

*A*s the result of colic, I meet many new parents shortly after their baby arrives. Usually, it is the dad with a cell phone to his ear. He has a distressed look in his eyes. The last few hours have been rough — colicky babies cry — and cry. By now, everything he and his wife have tried has not worked: holding, patting walking, whispering; holding, patting, walking, singing; holding, patting, walking — I have before me the visible half of a couple at wits' end.

First, I ask a couple of questions, just to make sure it is just colic. "Any fever? Twitching? Bowel movement?" I hand over a small bottle of infant simethicone.

"Will this make the baby sleep?" they always ask.

"Eventually," I say, "but first it will break up the large gas bubbles into a lot of small ones so your baby can pass them. Once the bubbles pass, the pain is gone and your baby will relax and sleep."

But there is another way. I explain what parents did before simethicone. "One parent would draw a warm bath and undress themselves and the baby," I say. "Then, while holding the baby they would sit and soak in the warm water while rubbing the baby. The warmth and touching relaxed the baby. Gas would pass and it was a bonding moment."

Of course, it sounds perfect. But few, I think, take this bath idea to heart. They are so stressed, and soaking in a tub just doesn't sound as powerful, fast, or convenient as a dropper of simethicone. This is how we treat stress. Instead of taking time to relax, we seek the quick fix with no fuss. And we begin to teach this lesson at an early age.

The Other Thing

It is 12:30 a.m. Two ladies and a man come to the pharmacy. The women are obviously mother and daughter. The resemblance is unmistakable: height, build, hair color and high cheekbones. As I approach, I can see that the daughter is obviously pregnant. The man is the daughter's age and stands a couple of feet behind her, off to the side. His face is framed by thin strips of long hair. I notice the smell just as I get to them.

"How can I help?" I ask.

"Do you have the thing to listen to the baby? "

"We have a stethoscope."

"Not a stethoscope. The other thing that doctors use."

"I'm not sure what that is. All we have is a stethoscope."

"Where can we find the other thing?"

"You might call a medical supply house or call your doctor's office and ask the nurse."

They turn and quickly walk away. No "Thank you," or "OK." They walk away. They are not rude, just focused on something else. The young man follows, hands in pockets, shuffling, waddling back and forth. The distance between them increases as they walk down aisle nine to the front of the store and out the exit. He quickens his pace to catch up, and I breathe in the heavy stench of cigarette smoke left behind.

A Lot of Pain

It is 10:35 p.m. We are busy — not overwhelmed, just busy. One technician is taking care of a customer at the front cash register. Another customer waits behind him. The other technician, who should have left five minutes ago, is still helping a customer at the drive-thru window. I am verifying and filling scripts.

A slender, muscular gentleman dressed in jeans, a dark tee shirt, and a long-sleeved unbuttoned shirt comes to the consultation drop off window right by me. I tell him we will be right there. He says, "OK." He is holding a lot of papers.

Being "right there" takes three minutes or so — longer than I would like. He is patient and when I greet him I say, "Thanks for being patient."

He holds his handful of papers up and asks, "These say I can't drink any alcohol; is that right?"

He does not ask this question the way it is usually asked. He is not half joking. He is serious. He knows the real answer is not absolute.

Strictly, I can only say if the manufacturer says no alcohol, then no alcohol. But he is right, there is a gray area. People drink and take medicines all the time. There can be risks, just as there are added risks to deciding to drive in bad weather. I call this a Dirty Harry question: "Do you feel lucky?"

"What are you taking?" I ask.

He shows me the papers. They are for three medicines: Prozac, Xanax, and Effexor. He has (at least) moderate psychological stress and it is not responding to single therapy. I can assume he has been treated for a few months (at least). This suggests some level of efficient metabolism of the products, which could, might, maybe, handle the addition of alcohol — some alcohol. Also I can't know for sure, but judging from his candid behavior I think he is showing me everything he is taking.

"You're asking me a question I don't have a guaranteed answer for. If I say yes, I could harm you. If I say no, you will anyway, without any guidance. What I can say, is combining these medicines with alcohol could cause additional drowsiness, sleepiness, confusion, and could interfere with breathing."

"Anything else?"

"What is he searching for?" I think to myself.

"How much do you want to drink?"

"A bottle of Jack."

"Over how long?"

"A night."

"I can't suggest that would be safe."

"How about a beer?"

"What do you usually drink, and how much?"

"A bottle of Jack a couple of nights a week."

"Do you have any liver problems?"

"No."

"If you just drink a beer that would be safer than a bottle of Jack."

"Thanks."

"You understand, I hope, that is still not a good or completely safe answer."

"It's what I asked for. Thanks," he says, and leaves. I wonder if he is suicidal and know he will drink more than a beer.

I watch him go. Why here, why tonight? Why me? His med sheets were not from RJ's and were not wrinkled, making me think his prescriptions were new. Where does he get his medicines? Where is he going to mix and drink — car, bar, hotel, apartment, home? I get a sense he will drink alone. I realize it is only Tuesday — already the week is taking its toll on him. I wish for a magic wand.

Years ago, a friend had a party. The next morning she noticed one of the guests had drank a bottle of vodka. "What kind of person drinks a bottle of vodka in a night?" she asked.

Her husband replied, "Someone with a lot of pain."

My thoughts and stare are interrupted when an elderly customer asks me to show him where the Pepto-Bismol is.

Sometimes, a pharmacy becomes a surreal place.

Sales 101: Insulin Syringes for Grandma

On the surface, it appears there are a lot of concerned grandchildren running errands for Grandma in the late night hours. They come to the pharmacy around one, two, and 3 a.m., always for Grandma, and never, never in my 33 years as a pharmacist, for Grandpa.

And all Grandma ever needs in these wee hours is "a ten pack of insulin syringes." She never needs Glucagon, or glucose wafers, or test strips, or lancets.

"Does she have an insulin prescription on file?" I ask. Some say she does; some say they aren't sure; some say she does but not at RJ's. Some say she doesn't need a prescription for insulin. I say she needs an insulin prescription on file to get needles from me. For some the game stops here. Others will offer a name and a date of birth which can't be found — hence, no needles. The problem must be my computer, they say. For some, the debate begins.

"Why do I need a prescription for needles?"

I say, "There is a high abuse problem in our area."

"But I don't need a prescription for needles," they argue.

"You do if I am going to sell them to you," I say.

They say, "I have bought needles here before without a prescription. (Notice Grandma has disappeared from the conversation.)

Another telltale behavior is for the "grandchild" to offer an overly enthusiastic "Hi!" the moment they get to the pharmacy counter, then immediately say, "How are you doing tonight?" feigning friendship and interest. They don't care how I am doing. They are trying to disguise their real intention with a Sales 101 technique.

There is no Grandma. The needles are for injecting methamphetamine or heroin, anything but insulin, and for anybody but Grandma.

No one gets needles. Most just walk away. A few yell, and even fewer accuse me of killing Grandma. Some pretend to be appalled, shocked, or in disbelief. Others complain to the night store manager. One lady accused me of being responsible if she got AIDS. I treat them with respect — let them save face. There is no reason not to. They are sick. I do not doubt this. They are a problem without an easy solution that should not be encouraged in the community I work in. I do not doubt this either.

I am a participant in the neighborhood where I work. If I cater to these "grandchildren," more, many more, from all over the area — not just the city — will come, and my neighborhood will be compromised. They will shoot up in their cars. Needles will be discarded in the parking lot or along the curb a block away. This happens when stores cater to the needle crowd. Saying no semi-protects my neighborhood.

Some pharmacists sell needles — no questions asked — as many (or even one) as the patient wants. This is their prerogative. They argue that to not do so will cause more disease and death. I just wonder if they live in the neighborhood.

Herpes and the New Boyfriend

*I*t's 1:30 a.m. Sunday morning. She is all over him. As I approach the pharmacy counter I laughingly think, "Get a room." They are mid 20-something. She is wrapped around and pressed against him. Wearing a tight top that slides down one shoulder, she is all angles and jewelry, dangling a sensuous posture that is eye catching. He is preppy. A solid brown belt separates his solid blue shirt and khaki slacks. His collar is buttoned, posture straight. He likes the attention, but clearly feels awkward that it is occurring here, now, in front of me. They are something of a mismatch, but sometimes opposites attract.

She hands me a prescription. "I need this filled," she says.

"Have you filled at a *RJ's* before?" I ask. "I don't think so," she says. I get her address, date of birth, home number.

"Are you allergic to any medicines?"

"No."

"Do you have insurance?"

"No."

"OK, give me 10 to 15 minutes. If you are going to wait in the store I will page you."

"We'll be here," she says.

I go to fill the script. It is for Valtrex 1 gram, #5; Take one a day. This is a dose, usually, for treating a recurrent episode of genital herpes. She has active herpes. She is infectious. And I am thinking he doesn't have a clue.

The Health Information Privacy Protection Act is a government sponsored and enforced set of regulations. It adds to and subtracts from healthcare delivery and receipt. As with many regulations, the intention is honorable, the effect is mixed.

I will also add that, as with many regulations, the effect is hardly benign, and rather malignant (i.e. it grows). It is another demand that due to its unnecessary complexity takes more away from the provider-patient relationship. Time is taken from the patient and spent in documentation with paperwork or computer keystrokes. Energy is taken away from the patient and spent toward CYA. In short, the attention given to patients (observation, talking and listening) is reduced and the result is a rushed reduction in quality. But the work had better be done. Government inspectors love "gotcha."

The main rule of HIPPA is say nothing about the patient, except to the patient. It means pharmacies are putting in private areas and phones at drive-thru windows. Because this is not completely private, rest assured, sometime in the future private areas will become more private and phones will have to be used by everyone in a drive-thru — adding even more to the expense and time to get prescriptions filled and healthcare delivered.

Sometimes, HIPPA is kinda stupid.

The upshot of HIPPA for the boyfriend is that I can't say anything to him about his girlfriend's (and soon to be his?) herpes.

My gut tells me this guy could get herpes tonight. Maybe he knows? Maybe not. Maybe she'll tell? Maybe not. He seems "new" to this relationship. Over the years I have filled a lot of scripts for herpes. More than once after counseling, I have had patients say they had no idea the other person was infected. Many wonder why didn't he or she say something. They say they never thought they would be buying this medicine (and not just now, but for the rest of their lives). More than once, I have heard anger and hate.

"Hope I Don't See You for A Long Time"

I was able to do nothing for all of these men and women, or for this guy — maybe. But there is HIPPA. Worst case scenario for me: she could report me to the Board of Pharmacy and/or sue. Worst case for him: a life-altering, life-time infection.

I don't have to page them. They do not wander around the store; they stay at the pharmacy counter. She is affectionate and unabashed, latched on to the guy. He responds in an awkward, not-as-experienced-in-such-a-public-display-of-affection way. I say her name to confirm the final act of getting the right medicine to the right patient, go over the directions, make a mention about nausea.

"I know," she says.

"Have you taken this medicine before?"

"Yes."

I tell her it is $65.00. She cocks her head up to her boyfriend, "Could you get this for me?" He is completely surprised. She whispers something in his ear. He is definitely caught off guard by her request, and whatever is said in his ear does not make the hand on his wallet any less confused. He has no clue. I said "Valtrex" when I mentioned her medicine earlier. He does not know Valtrex is for herpes.

He gives me the money. I give him change. As I staple the receipt to the sack, I say to the lady, "If you have any questions about your medicine or herpes give us a call." Usually I say, "If you have any questions about your medicine give us a call." I have added herpes in his presence.

She says she knows.

He hears "herpes" and is startled.

The Altered Script

It's 1:30 a.m. The drive-thru bell chimes. In the car are two men: one older, one younger. The younger man is the driver. He hands me a script from one of the emergency rooms. "Have you filled a prescription at RJ's before?" I ask. "Yes," he says. A few keystrokes, and I find him and tell him to come back in 20 minutes. "OK," he says, and off he goes.

The prescription is for generic Vicodin, hydrocodone, the 5/325 strength, 60 (sixty) tablets. But it is altered.

A zero has been snugly placed next to the "6." Also, a "ty" has been added to the "six." Physicians typically write the quantity to be dispensed with a number and also the number in longhand, a method to reduce altering. The ink is a close match, but not the same. It is from an emergency room far north of my store. This is another reason to be suspect. If a person is in pain, why would they travel past so many 24-hour pharmacies, especially with someone else who could drive? This happens frequently. People who do this must have the idea that somehow a far away prescription will not be checked. Have they forgotten we have telephones? What they don't know is that ER docs don't write prescriptions for large quantities. This prescription is for a 24-year-old male.

I'm not going to fill the prescription. I call the ER and check with the physician who wrote it and confirm it to be for six – just six. ER physicians often prescribe very small amounts if they suspect the patient is faking or up to some ruse. (Guess who pays for the ER charge? Answer: the person's insurance company, employer, or if they have no insurance or give a bogus address — *you*.)

"Hope I Don't See You for A Long Time"

Unless it is flagrant (for a large quantity, or for a C-2 script, like morphine, codeine, oxycodone, methylphenidate), I just tell the patient that the script is not valid; it has been altered. Some express a feigned surprise. Most just leave. They never ask me to call the doctor to confirm or call in a new script. They know I know. And I know they know I know. No accusation is made. If there is any further discussion, I just tell them they will have to go back to the doctor and get a new prescription. Some ask, "Can I have the prescription back, so I can show the doctor?" I tell them no. All they would do is take it to another pharmacy and try again.

Forged prescriptions are thrilling to catch. It's matching wits and winning. There is, I guess, an element of danger, but not much. Those who alter prescriptions are usually not violent and what tension might exist is minimized by politeness. It's not like a robbery — no gun against you. It's their wits against yours.

But there is a twist with this altered script. About a half hour later the older man from the car comes into the store. He walks up to the pharmacy counter for what turns out is his son's prescription. (The son, knowing the script is altered, has let his dad come in to pick it up.) I go to the father and say, "I did not fill the prescription. It has been altered." The father's shoulders drop and his eyes seem to bulge; a horrible gut feeling has been confirmed. For the first time, I see "crestfallen." I normally don't show the prescription, but he is so shocked, I say, "Let me show you." While holding the prescription toward him (and he makes no attempt to hold it), I point out the alteration. We are leaning toward each other over the pharmacy counter. "I checked with the prescribing physician. He said it was for six," I say quietly. "What happens now?" the father asks, not moving an inch. "From me nothing," I say. "I'm not calling the police." As a grateful father, he says, "Thanks."

Stunning Beauty, Startling Behavior

It is 1:30 a.m. She stands at the pharmacy counter and is stunning. She seems sophisticated for any neighborhood, especially mine, and especially for the graveyard shift. As I walk toward her, I am thinking she is one of the most attractive woman I have ever seen here or in any pharmacy where I have worked. Looks, posture, dress, jewelry — all connected. I think, "money."

"Hi, how can I help?"

"I need to purchase a ten pack of insulin syringes." She is polite, not overly polite as many who ask for a ten pack are. She is polite to the degree one would be asking for a pack of gum or picking up a prescription.

"Do you have an insulin prescription on file at RJ's?"

Her voice changes from polite to knowledgeable, "I do not need a prescription for insulin syringes," she says quickly.

"I do not sell insulin needles without a valid insulin prescription on file," I say.

Her posture changes into a stance. Her hands do not move from her purse. Her eyes do not leave mine, but the greeting has become a glare.

"I want a ten pack of insulin needles."

"You need a prescr—."

She screams, "I don't need a f@%*&#! anything to get insulin needles!"

"Hope I Don't See You for A Long Time"

Attractive has changed to horrid in an instant. She does not move her hands from her wallet or her eyes from mine. I stay where I am, ready to move if necessary.

Her eyes do not move from mine. "Get me the f@%*&#! needles." She says coldly.

"No."

Without breaking eye contact, she puts the wallet in her purse.

"You son of a bitch, you g#@ damn, son of a bitch." There is a final hateful look.

And she's gone.

Addictions mess up the beauty on the inside.

The Cursing

*I*t's Friday afternoon, around 3 o'clock. I am working the day shift, filling in at a different *RJ's* than my home store. The drive-thru bell chimes. This is an older *RJ's* store and the drive-thru window is one that slides open — no glass separates the patient from the pharmacy. It is great. You get to be outside when you go to the window. You get to feel the air, smell the rain, and when windy, get snowed on. You are also closer to the patient and it is more conversational, more personal, than the newer drive-thru windows that can't be opened and patients are talked to (more often talked at) using a phone.

The patient at the drive-thru is male, mid-40's, a bit chubby, and wearing a suit and tie. He has four prescriptions, all written today, by his cardiologist for moderately high blood pressure, irregular heart rate, and high cholesterol. One script for dipyridamole, a blood thinner. I check whether he has filled at *RJ's* before, and he has, but nothing like these medicines, just cold and flu stuff. I tell him 30 minutes. There are a number of people ahead of him. He's polite, says, "OK," and off he goes. We fill all but the dipyridamole. We are out of stock (OOS). I put in a quick order and will have it in the morning. No one likes OOS, but it happens.

Thirty or so minutes later, he chimes his way back to the drive-thru window. I go to the window with a sack containing three of the four prescriptions, slide open the window, confirm his name, and tell him we have three of his medicines and are out of stock on the blood thinner.

"Hope I Don't See You for A Long Time"

He goes ballistic, screaming at me through the open window. And because of the open window, his yelling fills the pharmacy and pharmacy waiting area. I listen. I say nothing. His response is way out of proportion to the situation. The cursing continues — you know the expletives. He goes on. I wait for him to run out of air. He continues, not hysterical; he is angry. His gestures mimic slugging actions, as if he is beating someone or something. He hits the steering wheel. Spit flies from his mouth.

As I listen, I hear his fear. Standing there with the sack of new medicines, all for his heart and life, it is easy to understand the mortality lesson he received earlier in the day.

All is not lost, my friend. There is much you can do.

3 a.m. Misoprotal

It's 3 a.m. She is quietly standing at the prescription drop off area. I had not heard her approach. "Hello," I say. She says the same and slides her prescription to me.

"Have we filled for you before?"

"Yes," she says. I find her in the computer: just a few prescriptions anti-inflammatory, and a couple of antibiotics over the last year. I tell her it will be 10 to 15 minutes. She doesn't say anything, just walks away.

Her prescription is for misoprotal; to be used as an abortifacient. She is pregnant. This will end the pregnancy. She has not had this before. The script was written two days ago. There has been a lot of thought given to this prescription before she decided to bring it in: second thoughts? She is bringing it in at this odd time on purpose, I am guessing, when no one else will be around.

Her posture is sunken, her voice soft. She is sad. She hadn't asked, "How long will it take?" which almost everyone does. They are impatient, in a hurry. She just walks away when I tell her it will be 10 to 15 minutes. She is not in a hurry. She wanders for a few steps, then comes back and stands at the pharmacy counter as I fill her script. She is not standing there looking at me, like some do, thinking it will make me hurry. She stares at a counter display. She acts like she has given up. I do all the double checks for accuracy. No one is ahead of her and the 10 to 15 minutes I told her it would take becomes less than five. I bring the medicine to her in a sack.

"Hope I Don't See You for A Long Time"

I ring it up. She pays. I counsel her about the possibility of nausea and cramping. She looks at the sack, hears a sympathetic voice, glances at me and says, "Thanks," and then looks at me for a millisecond longer. Her eyes are not tired, they are sad. "I wish you well," I say. She nods her head.

Three a.m. is not a good time to be alone.

Where Is "The Actress?"

It's 10:30 pm. Her sound arrives before she does, "Oh my ... Oh my ... Oh my ... ."

Then she appears at the pharmacy counter immediately falling to her elbows, prostrating her top half over the pharmacy counter with one or two more 'Oh my's'. Her voice has falseness to it. It is too constant for someone in so much pain — each 'Oh my' sounds like the previous one. The "oh my's' are evenly spaced. Her breathing is forced, to add some dramatic effect. Her arms and hands move too coordinated for someone in so much pain. Her head is bent down so she is looking at the counter. She has pushed her script in front of her. She is acting so she won't have to wait her turn.

Retail pharmacists see a lot of physical pain, enough to decipher real from portrayed.

We don't see the severe degree seen in ER's. We do, however, see a lot of just-dismissed-from- the-ER pain: broken bones, motorcycles road rashes, busted faces from fights, migraines, kidney stones, urinary tract, menstrual cramp, burns, hemorrhoid, toothache, torn muscle, cancer, eye injury, finger amputation from lawnmower, sore throat, headache, backache, gout, spider bites and dog bites. We may not always know what is hurting within the patient but real pain can be seen and heard when you are standing just a pharmacy counter away. I hurry real pain scripts through the work queue.

"Hope I Don't See You for A Long Time"

Retail pharmacists also see a lot of mental pain. We don't see the severe degree seen at home. We see the residue of depression, stress, and anxiety; we see the 'other place' look in the eyes, spent posture, tense mouth, mechanical motion and hear the numbed voice. At times, the pharmacy counter separates you from the cliché, 'still waters run deep.'

My 'Oh my' lady is waiting. I get her information: date of birth, address, allergy and insurance and tell her it will not be long. I tell her I will page her. She will not get scooted to the front of the line though. I will take care of her, as I would anyone else.

What is different is the way I talk to her. It is more clinical than personal. There is not as much tone of voice, not as much fluctuation. It is not rude. It is purposefully modulated to be in ... control not in ... fluenced. I am not leaning towards her instead am standing upright. Clinical is how to act when you want to send a message of being focused. When you don't want your focus to be distracted, it is appropriate to keep a distance so you can make decisions free of familiarity. Clinical is used also, I think, to move things along, so time is not used for chit-chat conversation. I am using CLINICAL TOV now so the other patients don't think she is going to get preferential treatment.

After finishing her script, I page my "Oh my" lady. She comes to the pharmacy a few minutes later with some groceries. People in real pain, especially physical, go to the chairs and sit. They do not have to be paged.

Sometimes, a pharmacy is a good place to meet a variety of people.

Plan B® — The Negotiator

It is 2 a.m. She stands at the counter, mid-to-late 30's.

"Hi," I say.

"I need a Plan B®."

I go to get it. When I return he has joined her at the pharmacy counter. I scan the box. It comes to $45.44. I am putting the product in a sack. No one else is moving: no purse, no wallet. I look up and she is looking at him. He is looking at the floor.

"You're going to pay for it," she says.

"We don't need it," he says.

"We are not the one who may get pregnant."

She continues to look at him. There is a stand-off. It is not too tense; neither person's body language is malicious. She is forthright. He is reluctant, and not where he wants to be. I want to grin. This is a "cute" moment. Cute, by definition, is anything that causes me to grin. I suppress this one.

The standoff continues. It gives me time to observe. I can see he is negotiating, even at this last awkward moment. He must be quite a negotiator. What is his strategy? Why did he wait until this moment to balk? He could have said no before they left the house, or in the car. He must know she gives in at the last moment. (Is this how he seduces her? "No, no, no … well … OK.") Just how good of a negotiator is this guy? I stand at the cash register as much a student as a pharmacist. Could it be that he is he just cheap?

Still there is no wallet, no purse. What is he thinking? She looks at him, arms now crossed. This impasse gives me more time to think. How did the "accident" happen that makes Plan B® a necessary digestive to the evening's feast? Broken condom? Loose condom? Didn't pull out? Didn't pull out quick enough? "Forgot" to put it on? I wonder if a Plan B® accident is like a divorce: rarely is one person completely to blame, and if so what did she do? He is acting sheepishly guilty.

Still no wallet or purse. He looks at the floor, then the counter, the floor, the counter, then quickly to her, then back to the floor, counter, floor. She continues to look at him.

"Don't keep this man waiting," she says.

"I'm not paying."

"Yes you are."

And he moves.

She gets piece of mind; he gets change.

Plan B® — An Errand

It is 2 a.m. Saturday. She is at the pharmacy counter, early 40's, dressed to party, lots of glitter, cleavage, red dress. She was here earlier in the week: last night or the night before. I can't keep nights straight sometimes. I come in at 10 p.m. on one day and leave at 8 a.m. on the next ... it is a little time distorting.

"I need a Plan B®," she says

I get one for her. As I do, I am checking my memory — I just sold her a Plan B® earlier in the week. I ring it up, put it in a sack, give her change. She offers neither conversation nor hint any is wanted. I don't exist. She is elsewhere with other things on her mind. She acts as though she is running errands: come home from work; go to the clubs; buy Plan B®; get milk; be home by three.

Sometimes, pharmacy is just a place.

The Arrest

It is Friday evening, 11 p.m. The place is popping. Yes, at 11 p.m. — phones, drive-thru, people at the pick up counter, and the two drop-off windows. In military terms, we are about to be overrun. Some have new prescriptions, some have new insurance, some have changes in their insurance, all requiring more time and all wanting it "Now." And they just keep coming.

More than one of us behind the pharmacy counter wonders, "Don't these people have homes?" Everything is sped up. "Hello" has been replaced with, "Have you filled at *RJ's* before?" Eye contact is minimal. Voices are a bit louder. Keystrokes are faster, sales are rung up and receipts are stapled, all with increased speed. (It would be nice to say with alacrity, but it is not pleasant; it is mildly brutal.) Sacks are stuffed in the rush, and nice gives way to efficient. Patients don't mind; they want fast. Scripts pile up. Waiting time has gone from 20 minutes to 30 minutes.

Two ladies, both nice looking, drop off a prescription for MS Contin 60mg #120. MS Contin is a long-acting oxycontin medicine. It is addictive and has a high abuse potential and a high street value. A lot of thievery and trickery accompany this medicine, at times making it a problem for legitimate users to get their prescriptions. This is a highly effective pain medicine. The prescription is a full page script — one that is generated from a physician's computer, all typed out, easy to read, and properly signed. Molly, a pharmacy technician, walks over to me with the script and says, "Would you look at this?" I look.

The first thing to look for are clues that this is a copy. If so, it is a forgery. You really have to look; printers are of such high quality now. It's not original. Around the prescription is a border that has a few flecks of white shining through and the borders seem a bit rough. This raises suspicion. The signature is not a copy. The ink is above the plane of the paper. It looks legitimate. We have a way to check. PJs' computer scans in prescriptions. So we can go into the system and pull up a previous script and compare the physician's signature. The problem is, we need a patient's name. We cannot just find a physician's signature by typing in the physician's name. We brainstorm, and in a bit come up with a patient that has gone to this physician before. We find a script with the physician's signature. It is very close. Maybe it is original? Then a discovery validates our suspicions. The physician is a psychiatrist. Psychiatrists don't write for MS Contin. They could, but it is not in their bailiwick of medicines.

We could tell the persons dropping off the prescription we need to call the doctor on Monday. They would probably want the script back. I would refuse and candidly tell them why. All this would do is tip them off. They may or may not make a scene. If they did, I would offer to call the store manager. But I am not going to give them this option. I am calling the police. I have two reasons: it is a C-2 item and the quantity suggests they are dealing. Altered scripts don't usually get the police called. I just call the person to the side and let them know the script will not be filled. And they go away. They know I know. They also know I am doing them a favor. Altered scripts for C-2s cross the line.

Now remember, we are being slammed: people, bells and phones. An out-of-earshot call on the phone is made to the store manager to call the police. I explain why. Now we have to stay busy (no problem) and not give any eye contact to the two ladies. If they get eye contact, they may figure their script has been caught and leave. Fifteen minutes later an officer shows up with the store manager at the opposite end of the pharmacy counter, away from the main dispensing area. He wants me to point out the two ladies. I do.

    The waiting area by the pharmacy counter is packed with people, 12 to 15 of them, some sitting, most standing — waiting, some more patiently than others. As long as we maintain our cool and stay busy, they seem mollified. Then, through this crowd come two policemen and one policewoman. The two ladies are dumbstruck. They did not suspect a problem. If they had, they would have left. Immediately, they panic. One starts to cry. The other tries to use her cell phone but is not allowed. The crowd at the pharmacy counter shifts its attention to the drama. Both ladies are crying now. One starts promising to never do this again: "Just let me go. I promise I promise." They are cuffed. The police keep the scene to a minimum, but certainly everyone in the pharmacy corner of the store gets an eye and earful. There is no joy in seeing them arrested. There is some pleasure in matching wits and winning, though.

    I am not making light of what happened, but after the two ladies were taken from the pharmacy, everyone waiting at the pharmacy counter was extra polite. Later, after the customers are gone, we all commented on how very friendly the patients had become, and there was talk of hiring actors to dress up as cops every Saturday night to come "arrest" other actors. Think of it as crowd control.

Laughter

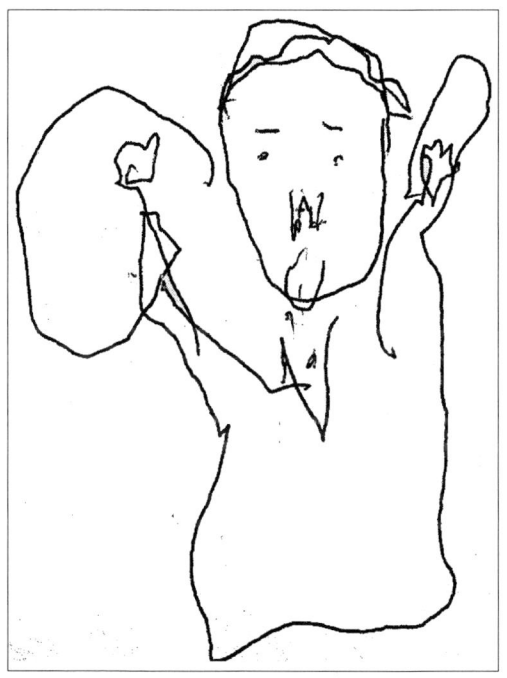

Portrait of Randall by Jaden Mobley age 7 ... who wanted to help with the book by being my official illustrator.

"Hope I Don't See You for A Long Time"

Randall J. Wright 42

Plan B® — The Road Trip

It's 3 a.m. The drive-thru bell chimes, and almost immediately the waiting button buzzes. (The patient's car rings the first signal. It is a chime. The waiting button is done by the driver's hand. It is a buzzer. It is easy to hate the waiting button when people drive up and immediately reach out their window and push it.) I come to the window. It is a couple in their early 30's. The lady is driving and she greets me with a smile, which at 3 a.m. is uncommon.

"Do you sell Plan B®?"

"Yes."

"How much?"

"Around 45 dollars."

"OK. We'll take one."

Plan B® is a restricted product, used for emergency contraception. It can be bought without a prescription, but has to be sold from behind the pharmacy counter. The buyer has to be 18 or older. I ring it up, go back to the drive-thru, tell them the amount. They pay. They are friendly. They are talking, laughing, animated, obviously into each other, and certainly night people. I have to interrupt them to go over the directions. I like 'em, even though a couple of moments ago they pushed the highly hated waiting button.

I say something like, "You two are the most awake people I have had here all night."

They laugh and say they are on a road trip.

"Where to?" I ask.

"Arizona, then who knows," she says.

"Hope I Don't See You for A Long Time"

The guy is leaning over from the passenger's side, smiling and nodding his head, looking up at me, not just sitting by the passenger door, uncaring or too cool to talk. Their behavior is contagious; suddenly it is a small party.

"You have a long drive," I say.

"Yes. We meant to get an earlier start, but 'something' belonging to someone got in the way," she says, tossing her right hand in his direction, pointing with her thumb.

Then he says, "Actually, she got in the way, too!"

She laughs, he laughs, and here I am at 3 a.m. laughing with them. And to think some people sleep at this hour.

"Drive safe," I say.

"Bye," they say, and off they go.

I return to the main pharmacy area and a minute later the drive-thru bell chimes again and again the highly hated waiting button is pushed. I go to the window and they are back, both with even bigger smiles.

"I thought you were going to Arizona," I say.

"Hey, we got to thinking we may need another Plan B® just in case. Can we buy another one?"

"Sure, no problem." I ring up the second Plan B®.

I say, "Let me see if I got this right ... You two are on a long road trip, enjoy each other's company, laugh a lot, and are having wild sex? I have to hate you."

They laugh. "Come with us."

"I can't, RJ's needs me."

And we all laugh.

3 a.m. Poem

There are things you can do during the night shift that can't be done during the day shift. You can listen a little longer to patients and take more time with questions. You can respond instead of react, and linger just a bit for conversation. You can have your own background music, a less hectic pace, say "Hi," and mean it, observe, and enjoy. And when your feet hurt, you can take off your shoes for a bit. You can also recite poetry.

Getting through the graveyard shift is a series of landmarks, just like getting through a day shift. The pace is much busier during the first two hours and last two hours: lots of patients are coming to the pharmacy counter or to the drive-thru window, and phone calls still come in at a brisk pace. The intervening six hours, however, are not as busy with patients or phone calls and are filled with tasks that one person can do and not begin to show signs of karoshi: finishing the work queue, doing daily deletes, updating the reserved/outstanding inventory counts, filling bins, cleaning up, doing compounds, the odd report, and so the night goes. Three a.m. is the halfway mark for the graveyard shift.

Not only am I working in the pharmacy, the night manager and clerk are out front, and I think, at times working harder than me. They see 3 a.m. as the halfway mark as well.

I like poetry, but nothing too sophisticated. I have memorized a lot from Ogden Nash, Shel Silverstein, and Mason Williams. A real crowd pleaser is from Mason Williams' Them Poems, especially *"Them Dog Kickers."* Google it. I like other poets as well, Shakespeare, and Greg Keith to name two, but they do not liven up the front staff and late night shoppers, like funny clever, short poems do. I reserve the more serious ones for my private use. Shakespeare's "Tomorrow" soliloquy usually gets muttered once a week, though it has changed in my mind from a lament to a prayer.

At or near three, I will tap the page button and announce, "It is time for the 3 a.m. poem. Tonight we have 'such and such' from 'so and so,'" and I recite the ditty. It is over in a minute. And the clock moves closer to going home time.

A few patients over the years have applauded and even come back to the pharmacy to stare at the odd acting pharmacist or to share the feeling.

Poetry, even at 3 a.m., touches the lucky.

"Is There Anybody Smarter Back There?"

The graveyard shift begins at 10 p.m. It's now Saturday night around 10:30. We are slammed: phones are ringing at their unnatural, stress-exacerbating rate; the drive-thru bell is (How do I say this politely?) chiming. When rings and bells fill the pharmacy I call it Quasimodo time. *"The bells! The bells!"* People are amassed at the pharmacy counter like wildebeest grouping to cross a crocodile infested river. Everyone behind the counter is doing their job. The chaos is being managed, and usually, by midnight things will be quiet. Until then, it's best to be on your game.

    I am at my station, the verification computer right by the drop off window, checking prescriptions and catching phone calls. This is an easy access point for patients who want to talk to the pharmacist.

    A wry, elderly black man appears. "Do you have V Power™?" he asks without any "Hello" or "How ya doing?"

    The suddenness catches me off guard and I say, "V Power™?"

    "Do you have any V Power™?" He says just as quickly the second time. He is not agitated, rather in a hurry. He is a man without an ounce of fat and no time to waste.

    "Well, I'm not sure what V Power™ is," I say.

    "It's for men." He says without pause or whisper. And with a quick motion pops his right arm up at a steep angle, mimicking an erection. "It's for men. Get it?"

    "I'm not sure if we have it," I say.

And without hesitation or any hint of rudeness he says, "Is there anybody smarter back there?"

Without pausing, I admit there surely must be and one of the pharmacy technicians finds the product for him.

Sometimes it's the velocity of knowledge people want.

Bipolar Lesson

After eight years working the same graveyard shift at the same *RJ's*, you get to "know" certain patients. They are regulars. You know their names and they know yours. Some are from the boats (floating casinos that dot a certain stretch of the River), some are dancers and bartenders from strip clubs, some are assembly line workers from the automotive plants, and some are just night owls. Almost all of these come in by 3 a.m. From three to five the store is quiet. There is time to have lunch and a break, finish what is left in the work queue from the day shift, and do reports and tasks. A lot can get done when you're not disturbed. The phones still ring at their abnormal forced rate, and patients from the four emergency rooms continue to trundle in, but all this comes at a can-be-handled-by-one-person rate in my store.

Throughout the night, insomniacs drift in, some seeking relief, some shopping. Others seek distraction. I call these wanderers. They are discombobulated; day is night, lying in bed is futile. They are not athletic, so 24-hour gyms are of no interest. They move like monks, without animation. Everything is done at a constant rate. There is no spark, just a barely discernable current. They don't come by and engage you in conversation, banter, or idle chit-chat.

Then there are the bipolar regulars, who have a very discernable current. Within an instant of seeing them, you can tell what "pole" they are in or have been for the last few nights. Quiet equals depressed.

Loud equals maniacal. "In between" is not often or long enough. They exhibit what is inside, vividly. Quiet or loud does not always tell everything, however. They can be quiet and be thoughtful, serene, angry, or fearful. They can also be loud and be thoughtful, serene, angry, or fearful. Their appearance reveals their poles, as well. Disheveled or neat is a matter of knowing them from years of meeting them. One gentleman is always dirty but at times not as dirty, which means he is feeling "up." One lady wears a lot of rings and bracelets, but when she is "down" she wears none.

I had one of my regular bipolar patients tell me, "This is the best horrible disease to have. The highs are great and the lows are just as much." He said this as he sat in his car at the drive-thru, left hand hanging just outside the window, flicking and wiggling his cigarette furiously. "Wow," I said. And before I could say more, "Gotta go," he said.

Retin A

*I*t is 3 p.m. on a Thursday. I am working a day shift at a medical building pharmacy. It is 1988. Retin A, an acne medicine, is new on the market and very popular with teenagers. It is also popular with women as it is used to eliminate fine wrinkles around the eyes — crow's feet. There is a lady at the pharmacy counter in her mid-to-late 30's, well-dressed, attractive, and petite.

"Hi," I say.

"Do you have Retin A?"

"Yes."

"Do I need a prescription for it?"

"Yes."

She lingers for a bit, looks at me, and says, "What could I offer that would not take much time so I would not need a prescription?" And she looks at me.

"I will need a prescription."

She says something short and polite-sounding, turns, and leaves.

I am befuddled. Did she mean what I think she meant — for a wrinkle cream?

Viagra®

He is in his late 60's or early 70's. He comes to the drive-thru window and gives me his name. He is picking up his prescription. The script is for three Viagra® 100 mg. It is late April, on a Thursday afternoon, about 2:30. Outside, the weather is perfect — one of those days too nice to be inside. I pull his prescription from the bin, go back to the window, and in the process of verifying his name notice his address is two blocks from the pharmacy. Just making conversation as we finish the transaction, I mention how close he lives and with the weather so nice how he could have walked to the drive-thru.

Looking at me, he says with a smile, "Gotta save my energy."

Both of us crack up.

Sometimes pharmacy is a battery — we store energy.

In Praise of Odd

You need a kook every now and then. They break the monotony. They give variety. They add colorful stress. A kook is someone with an eccentric behavior. You could be a kook. I, too, could be a kook. There are kooky customers, pharmacy technicians, pharmacists, dentists, doctors, physician assistants, nurses, hospital administrators, store managers, and others, to finish stating the obvious. Retail pharmacy has its share of kooky acting people, probably more than the Supreme Court and less than an adult book store. I could name names and tell stories

I've been in retail pharmacy long enough to understand kooks. I know where they come from and their purpose. They come from the mixing of events, history, societal forces, genetics and metaphysical goo much like the same ingredients that predictably give us criminals, or a Mother Teresa. Kooks have always been with us and will always be with us. In fact, if you are reading this in a public place, you are probably sitting close to a kook. And, if you are reading this alone, well … (Of course, you may also claim you are not a kook, just reading something written by a kook.).

Kooks are crafted into a trifecta of unexpected behavior, a "matching" appearance (in hindsight), and a "who-knows-what-goes-on-in-their-head" mystery. This concoction produces a look that is as coordinated as any crafted by the sophisticated senses of a stylist. Their appearance is coifed by the hysterical side of nature. And all the elements go together. They would make best selling Halloween outfits, but for their subtlety. (The wearer of such a costume instead of yelling "Trick or Treat!" would say "Surmise my disguise.") Only a connoisseur of people would catch the nuances and connect the telltale signs. Nowhere is this more evident than anyone wearing more than two rings on one hand. This is a tell-tale diagnostic sign of kookiness. It was pointed out to me by a physician friend. I have never seen it fail. (Remember, two rings per hand they may not be kooky, but more than two and kookiness lies within.)

Kooky people stimulate contradicting emotions: they are likeable and aggravating; frustrating and surprising. They make you want to look away, yet you can't. We have a guy, late 50's, who every time he comes to the pharmacy loudly orders his scripts to be filled by saying, "As soon as you can but just when you can; I'll just be waiting." And then he stands at the counter. (We have tried to get him to call ahead. It doesn't work.) While standing at the counter he talks nonstop about anything that comes to his attention: a fellow customer, a tattoo, a ball cap, what someone else is buying ("I like that soap too."), what one of the staff is wearing, the sound of the bell when the drive-thru is activated. ("That sounds like you got a customer at the drive-thru.") You can answer him or not; it doesn't matter, he continues on. You can interrupt him by talking to another person, but he will, count on it, join in. At times he gets attention from the other person, other times he doesn't. Again, it doesn't matter.

He is a kook because it is surprising to find someone so talkative at a public place. His monologue is odder than seeing a saxophone player by a subway ramp and a lot less odd than seeing a saxophone player in a subway bathroom. His appearance is designed to match his behavior. His hair is short, yet wild. It is spindly, twisting, spiraling and does not grow, rather shoots from

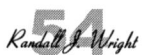

his face, head, eyebrows, and ears making his profile look like a primeval fractal. He has been expertly "coiffed" by the forces that compounded him. And should you wonder, he wears only one ring but has really long fingernails. (Could count as rings?)

He talks about his grandkids at some point every time. Once, while he was going on about them, the song about a woman being somebody's mother popped in my head and I realized he is somebody's granddad, and dad, and brother and husband. And while kooky, he adds to our store and it would be a lesser place without him, just as his home would be a lesser place without him. I like him, or if I was talking to you instead of writing I would say, "He's a kick," Which, says he is quirky and we all know quirky leads to kooky.

Once, late at night, about 2:30 a.m., another one of our kooky patients came in. I was not on my best behavior and was short with him. He got his prescription and left. Ten minutes later he called. I answered the phone. He began talking to me without introduction, assuming I would know him. He was right. He told me he is checking in on me; he could tell I was, "not yourself." Said he would keep me in his thoughts and be back. "No harm done," he said.

I was embarrassed, humbled, and barely uttered, "OK."

I read once that God chooses the foolish to confound the wise. That night the foolish were wise and the wise foolish, if I can give myself that much credit.

Sometimes pharmacy is a place where contradictions are a blessing.

Conservation, Not Salvage

It's 2:30 a.m. He always comes in on a Thursday — once a month initially, now once every three months — always on his way home from work. He has been coming in for seven years. He always wears blue jeans and a white tee shirt. Add a dark brown leather jacket in the winter. He is healthy, in his mid-40's. His chart has just two medicines — no cough, no cold, no flu, no blood pressure, no diabetes medicine — just two medicines for male pattern baldness. The first year it was Rogaine®, the last six, Propecia®.

He is friendly and will talk to you when you talk to him, otherwise all he says is his name and then, "Thanks." There were two episodes of confusion mid-last year on his billing. For the previous years he always got a 30-day supply. Then his insurance started allowing a 90-day supply. A couple of times his prescription was filled with 30 when it should have been 90. He never got upset, just said it should be for 90 and patiently waited while the quantity was corrected. Some get testy at such an error. He is stable, in control, calm, polite.

Like his clothing, like his temperament, his hair has never changed — there is no more, no less. The strands maintain a blond pullover on a shiny top. I see them clearly. He always writes a check and to do so he has to lean down, dropping his head slightly over the pharmacy counter. I know those strands. They are his personal barcode. Maybe he knows he is not growing any new hair, maybe not. Whether he does or does not, daily he takes his medicine to keep what he's got.

For a few years of our encounters, when he would lean over to write his check, I would see his blonde strands crossing his dome and would silently think, 'Let them go, so they can rest in peace.' Or, 'Go chrome, show your testosterone." However, his persistence has taught me he is the future of wise health care: conservation rather than salvage. Which may explain the lack of other medicines in his chart, his lifestyle is to take care of what he has, be it blue jeans, temper, hair or health. He is a beacon for all of us. Instead of losing what he has he protects, conserves what he has. This is a whole lot cheaper and safer and more effective than trying to replace or salvage what has been lost.

Sometimes pharmacy is a museum — we take care of artifacts

Coca-Cola Tattoo

*I*t's 1:30 a.m. She is a very attractive, early 20-ish brunette from the University. I am working at the 24-hour *RJ's*. She has a head cold and a revealing top. Her cleavage displays a Coca-Cola logo tattoo on the inner curve of her right breast. Why a business logo? I wonder. Why Coca-Cola and not Pepsi? Why the right not left? Is she planning on putting Pepsi on the left? Is it real or a stick-on? Does she have other tattoos? Where? All of these questions I want to ask, but instead I ask her questions about her head cold.

You have to maintain decorum.

No Answer

*I*t is 3 a.m. The phone rings.

"Are you a pharmacist?"

"Yes."

"I have a question that will require more than just a quick answer from you. Will you take the time necessary to listen to me?"

"I will give you what I can."

"I have a complicated question that will require a lot of explaining so you will understand what I am asking. This is why I need to know if you will take the time."

"I will give you what time I can."

She pauses. "This is a complicated question based on a person's unique chemistry. I am calling you at this odd hour thinking you will not be busy, so I can be thorough."

"Well, let's see what we can do."

"It will be difficult for you to understand the question if you do not listen to all of it."

"Let's see what we can do."

She starts, "Do you understand the neurotransmitter theory of depression?"

"I am familiar with it."

"I want to explain it to you as it affects me."

I am silent.

"Are you willing to listen to me?"

"I think your question would be helpful."

"It is not as simple as a question. You will need to understand my history before you can answer my question. This has happened before and I know from experience you have to understand my history or your answer will be the same as others."

She begins an explanation of the neurotransmitter theory of depression using some pharmacological terms: synapse, norepinephrine, and non-technical words (influx, tidal motion). She is articulate and methodical. She continues for a minute or two.

"Excuse me, you are giving so much information, it would be helpful if you would give me an idea what your question is."

With a hint of exasperation she says, "See this is the problem; you do not know enough. Yet, you want to answer my question."

I pause, then say, "I will not know the answer to your question."

She is surprised by my response. "No one has said that before," she says. And then, "I can't argue with that."

"I hope my time with you has not been an argument," I say.

"Good night," she says, her voice indicating her time has been wasted.

I hang up, prop my elbow on the divider that separates the dispensing area from public view, cradle my chin in my hand, and stare at the phone. I think of a lesson about the purpose of communication: "to improve the quality of the experience," and how that conversation was beyond my ability to do so.

Vasectomy Couples

*N*ote: for about a year, I managed a pharmacy in a medical building in the suburbs. It was a normal shift, 9 a.m. to 6 p.m.

They come on Friday afternoons around 3:30. The woman brings the script to the pharmacy counter; the man stays off to the back, either sitting in one of the chairs or propping himself up on a ledge. The script the woman presents is for the man and it is for the generic of Tylenol #3® — acetaminophen with one half grain of codeine. This is used for mild to moderate pain — like one might have from a vasectomy.

There is a steady stream (no pun intended) of vasectomy patients and their wives or girlfriends to many pharmacies every Friday afternoon. Typically, guys get "clipped" on Friday afternoon so they have the weekend to recover. The women take care of things. The guys act a bit fragile — their gait, the slow walk, shoulders down, all send a body language signal of "you-would-not-believe-what-I've-been-through" vulnerability. (There is the exception of one guy, who came in, almost charging, saying loudly, "I just got my tubes tied. Fill this ASAP." He got a grin: clever under duress.)

The script is filled, the patient's name called, and the three of us — wife/girlfriend, patient and me — meet at the pharmacy counter. The name is repeated as a final check to make sure the right medicine is given to the right patient. Then I talk about the medicine, say the name, and explain the directions. I tell him to take with food, and offer a caution about how codeine may cause constipation ("so drink more water, juice and eat more fruit"). I explain how codeine may cause drowsiness and slow reflex time.

"Hope I Don't See You for A Long Time"

By now, no one is listening. The woman may be listening a bit more than the guy, but not much. They just want to go. Then I mention that because this may cause drowsiness, "You should avoid driving and being around hazardous machinery like a vacuum sweeper or a dishwasher." They both pause. Then they get it. "Hey thanks," he says. She says something like, "Hey, wait a minute," or "Men!" Then I say this side effect can last for years. The guy laughs. His shoulders move up. He's on his way back.

New Skin

She and her boyfriend wait at the pharmacy counter. She stands with her right arm extended. He stands back. She is agitated — stretching out her right arm and talking to me even before I start walking to her. He says nothing.

"I've been burned," she says. And just below the bend on the inside of her arm is a raised, very pink looking burn the size of a quarter.

"Hot glue," she says.

"How long ago?" I ask.

"An hour."

I ask her what she has done for it. She put cold water on it. "Perfect," I say, as I come from behind the pharmacy counter. I say it doesn't look too bad and she can put on a mild antibiotic cream, which I am moving toward.

She and her boyfriend follow. Within a minute of her coming to the counter with her outstretched arm, the three of us are standing in the first aid aisle. While standing with my back to the antibiotic cream shelves, I show her a tube of antibiotic cream. As I hand her the tube, I explain that her burn is a small burn, not severe, and that this medicine will help it heal. She looks at me, obviously perturbed, letting the tube dangle from her fingers.

"I was burned by hot glue," she says, amazed that I cannot see how extremely severe and important her burn is.

"And," I reply, "what you need to do is just let your body heal it. Keep it clean, open to air, don't over bandage it, and put just a smidgeon of antibiotic cream on it throughout the day."

"This is all I need?" she openly questions.

"Yes. Your body will do the healing. You can put on the cream and take some aspirin or ibuprofen for the pain. You'll be fine."

Her boyfriend reaches behind my shoulder, pulls a product off the shelf and says, "Hey this stuff is called NewSkin. This is what you need; you need new skin to replace the burnt skin." She takes the bottle from his hand, glances at it while shoving the cream I have given to her back to me, looks at me, says, "Dah!" and walks away with the bottle of NewSkin and her much smarter boyfriend.

Never underestimate the power of a clever product name.

Maybe I should have said what an awful, horrible, terrible burn she had.

"Tell My Wife"

It is 1976 or 1977, and I am working in a locally owned pharmacy in a small town. Nicorette® Gum has just come out as a prescription product to help in smoking cessation. During the day shift, one of the local farmers comes into the store. Usually he is friendly, not jovial, but friendly enough to say hi if you say hi first. Today, he is not. He walks straight back to the pharmacy counter from the front door and I can see from his gait, face, and body language he is annoyed. I say, "Hi," and as he tosses the prescription in a spinning motion to the counter, he says, "Does this crap work?"

I look at the script. It is for Nicorette® Gum. It is not just his language that says he is not here to be friendly; he is defiant like he is looking for a fight. His tone of voice is pissed off, and so far all I have done is breathe. Just a morning ago we sat at the same oblong table at Mike's Café, with six to eight other guys drinking coffee, jabbing at each other, solving the problems of the world and rolling the die to see who was going to buy. Today, what little history we have is not enough to effect politeness. He is not outright rude, rather he is angry about something, someone. (It's not me. I am nothing more than an object of displaced anger that happens to be in front of him.) His "crap" remark tells me to just be clinical. No small talk, no friendliness — just business.

I leave the script on the counter where he has tossed it, look at it and say, "This will help you quit smoking if you want to quit smoking." He counters instantly, "What if I don't want to quit?"

"It won't work," I say. He comes back fast, like we are in a debate, "So if I don't want to quit, this is crap."

"It's not crap," I say, "It's just not what you need."

"What do I need?" he asks.

"To want to quit," I say.

He stares at me. He wants to say "bullshit." I can see it in his eyes, but suddenly he realizes I may be right or he remembers that we drink coffee together with the same group of guys most mornings out of five workdays, and instead of an expletive, he says, "Tell my wife," and leaves just as annoyed as when he came in.

As he heads toward the door, I pick up the script and pitch it in the trash. He will not change his mind. I know him well enough. There is at least that much history between us.

"Tell your own wife," I say to no one. "And tell her that you're addicted and afraid. She already knows you're bull-headed."

Food From a Machine

She never came into the pharmacy. I only saw her as I walked by her house, which I did five days a week, from the rural Kansas drugstore to the hospital. I never saw her inside a building — ever. When I did see her she was in her garden, which was also her front yard. She was thin, leather-skinned, 70-ish, and agile — a no nonsense lady. The only time I ever saw her stand still was when we talked, and that was never for long. It took two years for her to accept a conversation of any length from me.

She never came into the pharmacy (she said) because she took no medicines. During one of the few "lengthy" conversations (five minutes, max), I asked her how she was so healthy.

"Never ate food from a machine," she said, no further explanation given or expected.

Sometimes pharmacy is not what people need.

Randall J. Wright

Love

*Years ago, in a college writing class,
I was taught only three things are worth writing about:
life, death and love.
As I watch an elderly couple leave,
I see two of the three and hope the third is a long way away.*

"Hope I Don't See You for A Long Time"

Late Night Bikini

It's 3 a.m. A lady quickly walks through the corner of my vision just enough for my brain to register that she is wearing a bikini. This is not normal, even in my RJ's pharmacy. I walk over from where the corner of my vision ends and my full vision begins to make sure I've seen what I've seen. She is wearing a blue bikini. Darting up the aisle, then rushing back, she turns and heads up the next aisle, this time almost at a run.

"Can I help?" I ask.

She turns to me and begins moving her arms in wide gestures and with a hoarse voice saying she needs something for breathing. Her eyes are wide. Behind her comes her boyfriend from another aisle. "She's having an asthma attack," he says.

I quickly move from behind the pharmacy counter and over to the Primatene® Mist. Rather than just give her the product, I open the box and rearrange the mouthpiece. (The packaging is confusing and makes the panicky user panic a lot more when it does not "fit." I've seen an asthmatic tear open three boxes trying to get the inhaler to fit on the mouthpiece while screaming in hoarse panic, "These are defective!")

She immediately opens her mouth into a big "O," drops her head back, brings her long arms to her mouth, grasps the inhaler, and gulps down a puff of medicine. She sits in a nearby chair, doesn't move, and with wide eyes looks straight ahead, waiting, breathing with concentration and caution.

"I will watch you," I say.

She looks at me and says not a word. Air and energy are too precious to use on speech. Moving her arms in a wide sweeping motion — as if doing so will open her lungs — she takes a second gulp of medicine. She still breathes with caution — very controlled — wanting to keep as much medicine in as she can. Her eyes, wide open, are frozen in a controlled panic. She has had this happen before. Her boyfriend, off to her side, stands still. He has seen this before and knows less motion and less talk means less stress. All three of us just wait.

Ten seconds pass, then 20. By 30 seconds she begins to relax. She feels air in her mouth, her throat and her lungs. After a few breaths, her posture changes. She un-tucks her legs from underneath her chair; she sits for comfort, not life support. Within a minute her boyfriend is talking to her. He, too, sees the signs of air coming in, staying in, and air coming back out. She coughs — a good sign.

"If you're coughing, the medicine is working," I say.

She looks at me and nods once, still preserving every erg of energy. Her boyfriend sits beside her. She takes a couple more minutes to recover, her gesture of putting the inhaler in her mouth now not as wide-sweeping.

I go back to the pharmacy. A few minutes later she comes to pay. She acts almost solemn — another episode dealt with. She is clearly tired. They leave. A minute later, the boyfriend comes back to the pharmacy counter, and says "Hey." He is leaning over the counter with his hand extended. I come over. "Thanks," he says. We shake hands.

"You're welcome."

Life and Love

It's late, but not that late. It's 11:30 p.m. They stand together at the pharmacy counter. I'm on the phone. I look at them and raise my hand with my index finger in the air, indicating they will not have to wait much longer. They nod.

The call is done. I walk over to them. They are an elderly couple. Later, as I refill their prescription I see she is 75 and he is 78. They have two empty vials to refill.

"Give me 15 minutes," I say.

"OK," they say.

After taking their empty vials I move to the dispensing area. My attention is redirected to a computer screen. I enter the refills and make sure the scripts go through our double-checks for safety and insurance billing. This takes a couple of minutes. As I turn away from the computer screen I see they have moved to a row of chairs at the opposite end of the pharmacy waiting area. And there, sitting next to each other, they are holding hands.

Normally I try to get people out as quick as I can with attention to all the steps for safety and accuracy. However, this couple makes me slow down. I like being in their company. They are more than cute, they are magnificent. I start to walk over to them to say something funny or clever like, "If this lady is bothering you I will call security," but I stop. "Leave this moment alone, don't disrupt it," I think.

"Hope I Don't See You for A Long Time"

I finish filling their prescriptions, and go the pharmacy counter. They notice me as I call their name, and with some slowness they get up and come to the counter. I do all the stuff I am supposed to do: counseling, ringing the sale, finishing up the transaction. After all of this, I ask, "So how long have you two been holding hands?"

"Since seventh grade," he says.

"You do it very well," I say. They both nod.

Years ago, in a college writing class, I was taught only three things are worth writing about: life, death and love. As I watch my elderly couple leave, I see two of the three and hope the third is a long way away.

Sometimes pharmacy reminds us what is most important.

"Ms. Bardot, Would You Come to the Pharmacy?"

At times, retail pharmacy is very stressful. During a rush, which may come without warning (but can be counted on to happen every Monday through Friday from four to seven, before an impending storm, and after a local professional sporting event, the NCAA Final Four, or The Super Bowl), staff and equipment get slammed. Phones ring at a faster rate than home phones (some idiot's idea that this will increase patient service), drive-thru lanes fill, and people amass at the counter, some with new or changed insurance information, slowing checkout for everybody. This situation tests the best work-flow plan, people skills, and the patience of understanding as well as rude patients.

Staff must deal with this stress. The more experienced become more deliberate, the less experienced lose their people skills, hurry too much, waste motion, and send signals to patients they are losing control.

Bridget Bardot was, for me, THE sex symbol when I was a kid. (Jane Mansfield was popular as well, but not French.) Bardot caught my attention then and still has it now. When the work gets stressful, I pick up the phone and page, with just a hint of a plea in my voice, "Miss Bardot would you come to the pharmacy?" The experienced staff chuckles, the inexperienced staff don't notice it, I feel better, and patients never know.

"Hon"

*I*t's 6:30 a.m. The neighborhood is waking up. The phone rings a split second before the drive-thru bell chimes. I'm close to the phone and grab it hoping it is a quick call.

"Good morning, *RJ's*."

"I need to call in my prescription to be filled, Hon." The caller is an elderly lady.

"Do you have the prescription number?"

"Yes I do, Hon. It is …" and she gives me a six digit number.

"Who is this for?"

"It's for me Hon," and she gives me her name.

"And it is for …" and I mention the name of the medicine

"Hon, that's right."

"When do you want to pick this up?"

"Oh sometime this evening, Hon."

Some elderly women use friendly words: honey, sweetie, dear – like syrup splattering them on every sentence. But my caller is not Mrs. Butterworth. Her voice molds the word "Hon" in the most artful way to say it. There is nuance: at first formal, then friendly, then apt, then cooperative, then affirmative, and finally, gracious. Even though she uses it in every response it is not overdone anymore than using a period after each sentence is too much.

As our quick conversation nears its end, I feel like she has given me a nickname, nothing pedestrian like Yogi or Maddog, rather a term of intelligence — a real sobriquet.

I am under her spell, beguiled. She is a gift.

After all the "Hons" I say, "Thanks for calling, Dear."

Yep, I called her Dear. It just came out. I must have wanted to put a bow on the gift. Thank God it was a quick call, no telling what else I might have said. Now to the drive-thru …

"I Will Pray for the RT's Family"

"A professional cannot be provoked." I have forgotten where I read this.

Most of the time, I keep my professional behavior. A few times — in over 33 years as a pharmacist, I will say in my defense — I have not. And I confess, it seems like when I lose it, I really lose it. I let stress build. Usually the stress comes from the workload: so many people wanting so many prescriptions in such a short time with phones ringing, drive-thru bells chiming, insurance billing snafus, and ineffective government add-on procedures, all interfering, challenging, and compromising my goal of prompt, accurate pharmacy care. And nothing adds more stress to this frenetic pace than the fear of making a mistake: incorrect filling, not catching an important drug-drug interaction, duplicate therapy, incorrect dosage, drug allergy, etc.

During one of those stressful moments, one patient not only acted much better than I, he did more to teach me the lesson, "a professional cannot be provoked," than any other learning experience.

It is 12:30 p.m. I have been slammed since I came in at 10. My technicians left at 11, but the patients did not. It is hectic. The day shifts have been slammed as well, and a full night's work has been left in the work queue in addition to all the other graveyard shift tasks. The stress of getting everything done that I am responsible for is building. A patient comes in and within a minute or two our exchange at the pharmacy counter deteriorates. As he leaves he says, "I will pray for the *RJ's* family."

Ouch.

A clever and, hopefully, forgiving patient.

If he should read this, I apologize.

Birthdays

The quickest way for me to pull up your file is to key in your birthday. This will retrieve not just your file, but others with the same birthday. I look for you, find you in the list, highlight your name, and your chart appears. In just a few more keystrokes I can refill a prescription or scan in a new one.

Most people give their birthdays in a number format such as: 4-23-53. Some will say, "April twenty third nineteen fifty three." This takes longer. I prefer just the numbers; they are easier, faster. They are also more accurate; no translation is involved. I have often wondered why these people don't use the number format like everyone else. Is it their way of saying "I am more than a number"? Are they using the name of the month to attach importance to their birthdays, as if they signify something else? I think so. They are defying Shakespeare's "Tomorrow" soliloquy — they are saying we are not "poor players … full of sound and fury signifying nothing."

When I started in pharmacy I also thought birthdays were to be treated with some importance, even some regality — to denote that something important happened on that day, not just an accident. I would not say, "What's your birthday?" I would say, "May I ask you for your date of birth?" That was then. Now I have given in to the speed that is driven by volume. I only ask with such flourish when dealing with elderly women, the great-grandmother types. I know they see it as respectful behavior — the way they were taught to ask, if they had to ask.

Respect for birthdays notwithstanding, asking for birthdays is also a way to have fun. Sometimes after getting the birthday number from women, I repeat it back, moving the year 10 years ahead so 1963 becomes 1973. They like that error. They correct me with a smile. I say, "You could have fooled me." I know it's campy. They know it too, and they allow it. Timing is important. Too late at night, while they are in pain and tired, it is not funny. At the drive thru, early in the morning as they are on their way to work, it is perfect.

Birthdays can be fun with men as well. Just ask a guy what his wife's birthday is while she is standing beside him. Most guys know their wife's birthday, although some guys sweat a little. I remember one who sweat a lot.

They had been to the emergency room and came to the drive through about 2 a.m. He was driving as his wife sat beside him in the front seat. They were in a pick-up truck, so they were sitting high enough we were at eye level. He put her prescription in the drive through drawer. I pulled it in, did a double check on her name, and asked if she had filled at RJ's before. He said yes, and I asked him for her date of birth. He looked directly at me and suddenly his expression became a mixed reflection of bewilderment and panic, a deer-in-the-headlight stare. She cocked her head to listen. He physically swayed and stammered. His right hand tightened on the steering wheel, and he blurted out her birthday, eyes fixed on mine. It was quite a 10-second show. She laughed and said loud enough that I could hear, "You are so lucky!" Then he said to me, "Man, next time give me some kind of warning. Pass me a note or something!" We had a good laugh.

Sometimes as I dash in a birthday on the keyboard certain dates catch my attention. At those born in 1975, I take a quick glimpse. While they were just coming into the world, I was just coming out of pharmacy school. It is an odd reflection that I

haven't clarified, but as I quickly look at them I wonder, "Are they what my career looks like?" One lady who comes to the pharmacy was born on January 20, 1968. I smile at that date every time it comes up. This is the day I first kissed a girl. It was in a church parking lot, a Saturday, at 12:55 p.m. (We are still friends, though she doesn't remember the kiss. "If you say so," she says.) Another lady who comes into the pharmacy was born February 9, 1979. My best friend was killed on that day in a fire. He was a fireman. I always take a glimpse at her, and think of Ade and how much time has passed. He has a cool nephew. When I see people with my birthday or year of birth I glimpse at them as well. Do I look that old? I know, I know, I should pay more attention to pharmacy matters, be more clinical, but now and again I slip.

Sometimes pharmacy is a place filled with birthdays, not medicines.

"I'll Wait"

*I*n December of 2006, I was diagnosed with Parkinson's. Suddenly, I existed on both sides of the pharmacy counter: pharmacist on one side and patient on the other. I remember just staring at a bottle of Azilect® on the shelf and thinking, "Will you help enough?" My faith in medicine got a test.

A few weeks later, just 10 minutes before my 10-hour graveyard shift was over, an elderly gentleman came to the pharmacy counter to pick up his medicine. His insurance had changed and he was trying to get his new insurance card out of his wallet. His hands were shaking. The more he tried, the greater they shook. Eventually, he put his wallet down on the counter, and held it in place by leaning on it with the palm of his left hand. With his right hand now shaking even more, he tried to grab the plastic insurance card. He missed repeatedly. His shaking was due to Parkinson's. I just stood there, seeing my future.

With a low voice, he cursed at the card, shook some more, then quietly cursed again. A few seconds later I said, "Let me get this for you."

"No," he said, "I'll get it."

"Take your time," I told him. "I'll wait." And I quietly cursed Parkinson's with him.

How Many Pills Will I Live?

Nothing reminds one of mortality like routine.

Pharmacy is filled with routine. It helps with accuracy and workflow. Prescriptions are filled in a certain sequence so safety checks are performed. Orders are put away the same day they are received. Controlled substance counts, daily deletes, and frequent inventory measurements are done. Insurance claims are submitted, corrected, updated, or deleted.

The typical work day consists of: do this and this, then take a break; do this and that, then take lunch; do that and this, then take a break; do that and that, and then go home so tomorrow you can do it all over again. Routine sets in, and days, then weeks, then months slide by with increasing momentum until holidays merge into one big, incessant calendar of doing the same thing day in and day out.

While pill counting is done more and more by machines, hand counting still occurs. After watching months and years go by, one day it happens: you're counting pills on a tray and the question comes to you — How many pills will I live? You count out how many represent your present age, you stare, and add five more, then five more. Like a fortuneteller throwing out bones, you pour out more pills and count, thinking, "Is this the number of years I will live?" Then you laugh, and say out loud, "I need to get a hobby," and the tech or pharmacist next to you says, "What did you say?" and you say, "Nothing, just wasting valuable time."

13 Medicines, 39 Pills

She is 73 and takes 13 different medicines a day, for a total of 23 pills a day.

He is 68 and takes 18 different medicines a day, for a total of 27 pills a day.

Another "he" takes 15 different pills a day, for a total of 22 pills a day.

Another "she" takes 12 different pills a day, for a total of 23 pills a day.

A family member usually picks up the medicines. When they call in their orders it is a long list. I have come to know their voices. Most have adult onset diabetes. They usually take two oral medicines, some with insulin. All have high blood pressure, some with potassium depletion. They take sleeping pills, anxiety pills, a pain medicine, and sometimes inhalers for asthma. Their orders fill a #10 sack (which is 4 1/2" x 12" ... big!).

Years ago, a patient asked, "How do all these pills know where to go?" I popped back with, "They're barely trained. So they go everywhere they can."

To see so many vials and pills being dispensed for one patient at one time is when I feel that I am merely in charge of accuracy, not simplicity, or safety, or effectiveness. I am fulfilling the role of a good technician more than a pharmacist with interpretative knowledge and experience. The pharmacology not only dwarfs me, it dwarfs everyone involved. With so many different kinds of pills, and so many of each, all going everywhere they can, no one can claim to understand all that is going on inside the "machine" of Mark Twain's "What is Man?" Accessibility and vigilance are good mechanics: taking the time to listen to patients or their family members and question them for clues of side effects or interactions. Even with taking time, listening, and questioning, one has to make two assumptions: 1) a good medical history has been taken and 2) good follow-up is being done.

Bold prescribers with their backs to the wall prescribe so many medicines in an effort to help patients. Hopeful patients with their backs to the wall want to hold on to what is left and take them. Still, I am sure some patients take more than they need, whether their medicines fill a #10 bag or just one bottle. It is not the place of a pharmacist writing a vignette or for anyone who is not directly involved with the patient to say how much is too much. The patient should get that answer from the doctor. All I can offer is a guide when patients say they want to take less. "Tell your doctor," I say. "And when you do, know that he may well ask what you are willing to do to take less. Diet? Exercise? Stretch? Socialize? You have to do more than just say, 'I want to take less.'" They nod agreement, but most (You can tell by the very slight nod.) don't like my answer. The very lack of helpful (read: healthful) behaviors that got them in trouble are the actions they don't want to change. I understand.

In my first class, on the first day of pharmacy school, the dean came in to welcome us. He finished by saying the most fundamental use of medicine is to use the least amount of medicine for the shortest period of time. As crazy as this may seem to say: the least amount for the shortest time is for some a #10 bag of medicine. It can be less — if hopeful patients act bold and add helpful habits.

Sometimes pharmacy is a place where the pharmacist lectures.

Air Hunger

*P*rescriptions are usually written with the reason as part of the directions, such as: take one tablet every six hours as needed for pain, or take one capsule a day for depression. Most directions are unspectacular: you expect a pain medicine to be used for pain, or insulin for diabetes.

One medication, however, has directions which are not so unspectacular. This medication is Ativan solution. Ativan is typically used for stress or agitation. It can also be used for air hunger, which is a unique form of agitation. The directions usually read, "Give one — two mls every 1–2 hours as needed for air hunger."

Ativan is given at the last stage of death. The patient is most likely dying from a cancer. When filling this prescription, I can't help but slow down and handle it with a bit of reverence. Suddenly, the noise and controlled chaos of a retail pharmacy becomes background and everything else is minor. I hurry the script through the work queue, and skip it to the front. Someone, a family member or a hospice nurse, is usually waiting at the pharmacy counter. I do the typical double-check for accuracy.

A thought is given about a life spent or a quick prayer. A glance is given at the age. A look at the chart: Do they have a spouse still living? Family to be with them? May God bless.

The Last Prescription

People don't always pick up their prescriptions. The reasons are many: price, they get better, insurance expires or won't pay, they move, or they transfer to a different pharmacy. And some die.

Sometimes the family sends a card thanking the pharmacy staff for helping. Or they call. "Dad died last week. Would you take him off the automatic refill list?" When I get these calls or letters, if I know them well enough, I wish them well and ask them to tell me a story about their dad or mom or spouse or partner. There is always one story. I have never done this for a child's passing. I can't. I know there is a story, but I know I couldn't keep my composure to tell one about my nieces or nephews, so I don't ask. I just go to the computer and close the file. I look at the last prescription they got filled.

Was it for a new condition?

Continuation of what was being treated?

One with serious side-effects? Did the treatment last a long time?

Did they get a full prescription or a partial, as if they knew the end was close?

Would it have been a medicine they would have given themselves or did someone else open the bottle, and shake out the last pill?

Who poured the last glass of water?

Was it just a sip?

Take Care

*I*n spite of the title and opening story — I don't always say, "Hope I don't see you for a long time," at the end of each dispensing. Most of the time it is, "Take care" or "Drive safe." These are quick and heartfelt goodbyes. A lot of people who come into the pharmacy didn't take care of themselves, so "Take care" is obvious. It doesn't take being a pharmacist to know about people dying or being maimed in accidents every day, so "Drive safe" is obvious as well.

I say "Congratulations" to parents when they bring in a child with a broken bone from sports or just playing. Most kids should be active enough that they break a bone, ideally a clean break, not a compound or worse. Fractures and a fat lip from missing a fly ball also get a "Congrats." The parents get the praise — they have not raised a couch potato. Sometimes I will ask the kid, "Did you have fun?" Most nod or shrug a "Yes." Then I say, "Cool."

On occasion, I will, after helping out a new dad, finish by saying, "Be a good dad." They like that. Many respond, "I will." They are so full of the future.

On the fifth of July a few years ago, at about 2:30 in the morning, a young guy in his early 20's came to the pharmacy counter. His face was blackened, his lips huge, much bigger than Mick or Bianca's; they were busted with large splits, eyes black and blue, his tongue swollen. I assumed he had been in a fight. He was talkative, but not easily understood. It took awhile to get his information. After filling his pain medicine and just before my,

"Take care," he said, "Sparklers." He then told me how he had held four or five in his mouth then lit them. They exploded.

"I didn't know they would do that," he said. "Did you?"

"No," I said, "I did not."

Then I said something I've never said in a pharmacy. I told him, "Good luck."

"Thanks," he said.

He should have said, "Amen." I meant it as a prayer — as in, "I pray you don't win the Darwin Award later in life."

Sometimes pharmacy has no simple good-byes.

At Peace for a Day

I think I just had my first drug experience. I'm not counting alcohol or the Paloma Picasso perfume a waitress was wearing a few years ago.

What I had was an overwhelming feeling of being at peace. I'm sure there is a greater medical term, fancier, but three days after starting Sinemet for Parkinson's, I had the unmistakable feeling of being at peace. It was not a surge, but more of a glow. I would certainly recommend it.

I was not one with the universe, and everything did not suddenly make sense. I did not see how I fit into God's plan. It was not cathartic; I did not weep. I was merely content and clear-headed. Birds didn't chirp louder, the sun was not brighter, my normal was everywhere around me, and that was just fine. I didn't laugh and I didn't call anyone to tell them. I walked around the house, read some old favorites and discovered some new "stuff." I sat, I enjoyed my thoughts, and I let the feeling have me.

It lasted a day. Next morning I was back to normal: doing a sine wave from angst to happiness to angst, feeling the pressure to get things done, feeling behind. Three weeks later, because it didn't happen again, I stopped my Sinemet for 2 weeks, then restarted, hoping the feeling would return. It has been ten days now with no repeat. I guess I'll just have to have Parkinson's without the magic.

Still, three times a day, every time I take my Sinemet I think, "Come again, stay awhile."

Acknowledgements

These stories have stumbled around my head and heart, some for years. A number of people are responsible for getting them out and onto paper.

Bob Mobley went from a grammar checker to just the right person, at the right time, to say the right words. Then one night at book club with Jim and Ruth Siress, Sally and Paul Jenkins, Dan and Sherri Cram, Shawn and Conrad Jones, Anne and Chris Jones, and Claudia Wellman, he asked me to read some of my stories. They all listened, read, commented, and encouraged.

My good friends, Chris and Pam Bacon said they enjoyed them, Chris in his understated way and Pam in her effusive way. Then my sister-in-law Carolyn went superlative on me. Sheila Connolly, a pharmacist and friend, nodded her approval.

All this time, my friend Jean Dreiling would read them, sometimes just as I finished them, offering encouragement and a couple of spot-on suggestions. And my friend, Gretchen Robinson after getting a few rough copies via late-night e-mail, called early the next morning! Maggie Choplin liked them (no small recognition due to her healthcare background and being a long time friend). Valerie Stallbaumer, my longest friend, told me to write more.

Then Janet Conner, the only professional writer I know, after editing a number of the stories sent an e-mail: "I've enjoyed reading your book." Whoa. I almost went out and bought a beret, scarf, and a bottle of absinthe.

Sue Breckenridge, on more than one occasion, has taken what I have written and made it look like it is worth reading.

And all of these people would never have read what they did had it not been for Recie Mobley. Everyone should meet a Recie if they want to develop additional skills. First it was speaking, now it is writing. Thanks, Recie.

Randall Wright, R.Ph.

Randall Wright

Randall Wright, a pharmacist by degree ... and a keen observer of human nature and a master with words. He has a unique sense of humor and masterfully tells stories that let us see the world from a new point of view. His life has been a journey of owning health care and non-health care businesses. He is a health care advocate and has hosted radio pharmacy programs and has been a health care columnist in Kansas City. He has served on the National Council to Prevent Health Care Fraud and Abuse and was the first pharmacist to judge Patient Education Awards for the American Academy of Family Physicians. Randall has also published numerous business and technical articles and books. He is passionate about quality healthcare and inspires excellence.

Pharmacist, author and international speaker, Randall has presented in excess of 1,500 seminars, keynotes and workshops. He knows how to light a fire in his audience that inspired personal growth. Randall mixes energy, passion, fun and lots of practical knowledge, with an engaging style that keeps his audiences learning, motivated ... and commenting on how much they enjoyed the day. You will enjoy **Hope I Don't See You For A Long Time"** his view of life from **"Over the Counter."**

Hope I Don't See You For A Long Time

Who hasn't been to a pharmacy? Across the counter, within the noise, the chaos and standing in line ... there is humor, bittersweet moments, heartbreak, deception, crime, fear, anger, characters, surprises, revelations, sex, life, death and love ... all the elements of a good read.

Enjoy Randall Wright's, **I Hope I Don't See You for a Long Time** to see the human side of a pharmacy. A retail pharmacy has depth, texture, drama and is not as sterile or as simple as many think. Enjoy and share with your friends.

I hope you enjoyed the stories of RJ's Pharmacy.

I invite you to share with me any questions, comments or thoughts by contacting me at:

> **Summit Speakers, LLC**
> **Randall Wright**
> 5333 Mission Road
> Fairway, KS 66205

Email: Randall@summitpress.biz

Websites: www.summitpress.biz

Visit **summitpress.biz**